Your hands made me and formed me.

Psalm 119:73 NIV

Bella Klaire Harris

Jamie + Matt Harris
Presented to

Tim, Brandy, Harlie + Annastyn Meeks
Presented by

July 14, 2018
Date

Congrats on
y'alls precious
miracle!
♡ - The
Meeks

The first handshake in life

is the *greatest* of all:

the clasp of an *infant*

around the *finger* of a parent.

It's a GIRL

Celebrating the Arrival of Your Newborn

SPIRIT PRESS

It takes *three*
to make a *child*.

E. E. Cummings

You created my inmost being;
you knit me together in
my mother's womb.

Psalm 139:13 NIV

When you look at a *baby*, it's just that:

a body you can look at and touch.

But the *person* who takes shape within

is formed by something you can't see and

touch—the Spirit—and becomes a living spirit.

John 3:6 THE MESSAGE

Beloved, if God so loved us, we also ought to love one another.

1 John 4:11 NKJV

I *love* these little people,

and it is not a *slight* thing when they,

who are so *fresh* from God,

love us.

Charles Dickens

The LORD your God is with *you,*

he is mighty to save.

He will take great delight in you,

he will quiet you with his *love.*

Zephaniah 3:17 NIV

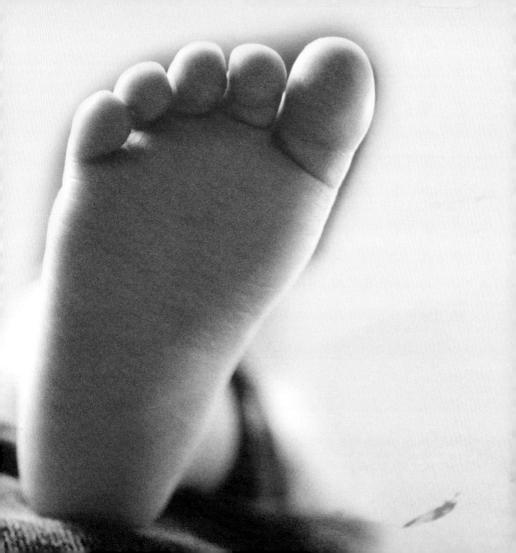

A baby's feet, like *sea-shells* pink,

Might tempt, should Heaven see meet,

An angel's lips to *kiss*, we think,

A baby's feet.

Algernon Charles Swinburne

my sweet girl

Sweet babe, in thy face

Soft desires I can trace,

Secret joys and *secret* smiles,

Little pretty infant wiles.

William Blake

Only a *baby* small,
Dropt from the skies;
Small, but how dear to us
God knoweth best.

Matthias Barr

As the heavens are higher than the earth,
so are My ways higher than your ways.

Isaiah 55:9 NKJV

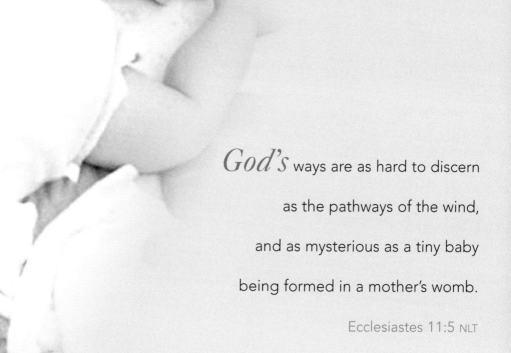

God's ways are as hard to discern

as the pathways of the wind,

and as mysterious as a tiny baby

being formed in a mother's womb.

Ecclesiastes 11:5 NLT

A baby: the tiniest thing
I ever decided to
put my whole life into.

I live my life in this earthly body
by trusting in the Son of God,
who loved me and gave
himself for me.

Galatians 2:20 NLT

Like a warrior's fistful of arrows

are the children of a vigorous youth.

Oh, how blessed are you parents,

with your quivers full of children!

Psalm 127:4–5 THE MESSAGE

my sweet girl

To a father, nothing is more *sweet*

Than a daughter.

Boys are more spirited, but their ways

Are not so *tender*.

Euripides

We find a **delight** in the beauty

and happiness of children

that makes the **heart** too big

for the body.

Ralph Waldo Emerson

Don't you see that children are GOD'S best gift?
the fruit of the womb his generous legacy?

Psalm 127:3 THE MESSAGE

One for a tangle,

One for a curl,

One for a boy,

One for a girl,

One to make a parting,

One to tie a bow,

One to blow the cobwebs out,

And one to make it grow.

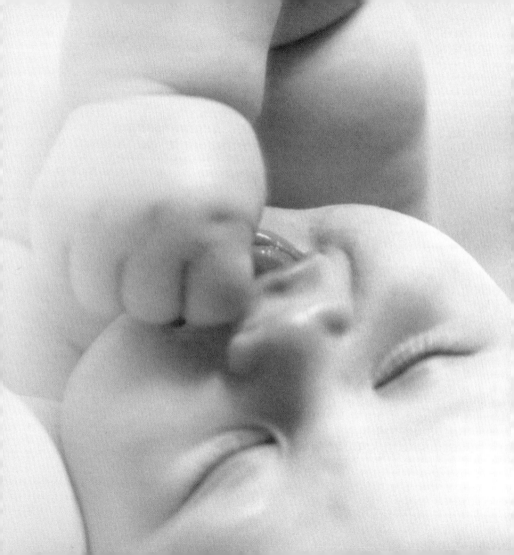

A man finds out what is meant by a

spitting image

when he tries to feed cereal

to his **infant.**

Imogene Fey

GOD, brilliant Lord, yours is a household name.
Nursing infants gurgle choruses about you;
toddlers shout the songs
that drown out enemy talk.

Psalm 8:1–2 THE MESSAGE

Jesus said,

"Let the little children come to me,

and do not hinder them, for the kingdom of heaven

belongs to such as these."

Matthew 19:14 NIV

The works of the LORD are great.

Psalm 111:2 NKJV

Baby: Unwritten **history!** Unfathomed **mystery!**

Josiah Holland

my sweet girl

Little arms and legs

dangle aimlessly in four directions,

appearing to be God's

afterthoughts.

James Dobson

If **children** grew up

according to early indications,

we should have nothing

but **geniuses.**

Johann Wolfgang von Goethe

Every *baby* born into the world

is a *finer* one than the last.

Charles Dickens

Many daughters have done well,
but you excel them all.

Proverbs 31:29 NKJV

my sweet girl

Some think the silky curls

And plump pink cheeks of a little girl

Bring more bliss to the old home place

Than a small boy's little freckled face.

Now which is better, I can't say,

If the Lord should ask me to choose today.

If he should put in a call for me

And say, "Now what shall your order be,

A boy or a girl? I have both in store—"

I'd say with one of my broadest grins,

"Send either one, if it can't be twins."

If properly fed,
the relationship between a mother
and daughter will bloom
into an eternal **friendship.**

Vivian Booth

Like mother, like daughter!
Ezekiel 16:44 NKJV

When a woman gives birth,

she has a hard time, there's

no getting around it. But when the

baby is born, there is joy in the

birth. This new life in the world

wipes out memory of the pain.

John 16:21 THE MESSAGE

Babies are such a *nice* way

to start people.

Don Herrold

Whatever is good and perfect
comes to us from God,
the Creator of all light.

James 1:17 TLB

Before I was born

the LORD called me;

from my birth he has

made mention of my name.

Isaiah 49:1 NIV

What are little girls made of?

Sugar and spice

and everything *nice;*

That's what little girls are made of.

A *rose* with all its sweetest leaves yet folded.

Lord Byron

I will praise You, for I am fearfully
and wonderfully made.

Psalm 139:14 NKJV

Monday's child is fair of face,

Tuesday's child is full of grace,

Wednesday's child is full of woe,

Thursday's child has far to go,

Friday's child is loving and giving,

Saturday's child has to work for its living,

But a child that's born on the Sabbath day

Is fair and wise and good and gay.

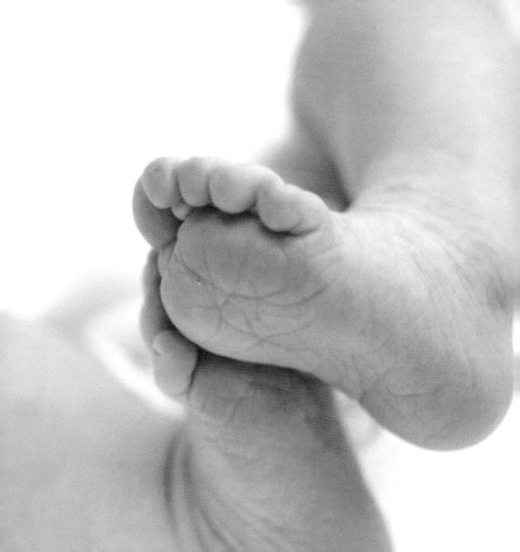

It's a Girl
ISBN 1-40372-026-6

Published in 2005 by Spirit Press, an imprint of Dalmatian Press, LLC.
Copyright © 2005 Dalmatian Press, LLC. Franklin, Tennessee 37067.

Editor: Lila Empson
Compiler: Snapdragon Editorial Group, Inc., Tulsa, Oklahoma
Design: Diane Whisner, Tulsa, Oklahoma

Printed in China

05 06 07 LPU 10 9 8 7 6 5 4 3 2 1

14945